everybody say

↳ CHEESE!

MERRY CHRISTMAS

ROBERT EARL KEEN

FROM THE FAMILY

PUBLISHED BY DANCE FLOOR BOOKS / NASHVILLE, TENNESSEE

PUBLISHED BY DANCE FLOOR BOOKS, NASHVILLE, TENNESSEE, AND DISTRIBUTED
BY RUTLEDGE HILL PRESS, P.O. BOX 141000, NASHVILLE, TENNESSEE 37214.

PHOTOGRAPHS ON ENDSHEETS AND PAGES 54-55 COURTESY OF ROBERT EARL KEEN
PHOTOGRAPH OPPOSITE TITLE PAGE COURTESY OF ROBERT EARL KEEN
PHOTOGRAPH ON FRONT COVER, PAGE 3, AND PAGES 44-45 BY JERI GLEITER (FPG)
PHOTOGRAPHS ON PAGES 6, 16 (CHILDREN), 18, 20, 30-31, 36-37, 41, 52-53, 62,
66-67, 70-71, AND 72 BY JIMMY ABEGG
PHOTOGRAPH ON BACK COVER AND PAGE 11 AND ALSO PARTIALLY USED ON
PAGES 10, 36, 52, AND 70 ©1996 BY JOHN HENLEY AND LICENSED BY THE STOCK MARKET
PHOTOGRAPH ON PAGES 14-15 ©1998 BY JOHN HENLEY AND
LICENSED BY THE STOCK MARKET
PHOTOGRAPHS ON PAGES 16 (THE MAN), 24-25, 28, AND
70-71 (FISHERMAN) BY BUNNY SNOW
PHOTOGRAPHS ON PAGES 17, 26-27, 48, AND 68 LICENSED BY PHOTODISC
PHOTOGRAPH ON PAGE 19 COURTESY OF LYNNE GREENAMYRE
PHOTOGRAPHS ON PAGES 22, 32, 33, 58-59, 64-65, 69, AND 70-71 BY HEATHER DRYDEN
PHOTOGRAPH ON PAGE 38 BY CAROLYN BLANKENSHIP;
USED WITH PERMISSION OF JAMES WHITE, THE BROKEN SPOKE, AUSTIN, TEXAS
PHOTOGRAPH ON PAGES 46-47 BY TONY STONE IMAGES
PHOTOGRAPHS ON PAGES 50-51 AND 63 BY HEATHER SWAIN
ALL PHOTOS USED BY PERMISSION.

RECIPE ON PAGE 9 OF "EGG NOG FROM HELL" AND PHOTOGRAPH ON PAGE 19
COURTESY OF LYNNE GREENAMYRE, ALSO KNOWN AS "LURLENE THE TRAILER COURT QUEEN."
PHOTOGRAPH TAKEN BY MARY BLAKLEY, MINISTER OF PROPAGANDA.
FOR BOOKINGS, E-MAIL TO LURLENE@LURLENE.COM.

LOCATION CREDIT: D + N CAMPGROUND,
100 OLD RIVER ROAD, ASHLAND CITY, TENNESSEE 37015

DESIGN BY JACKSON DESIGN, NASHVILLE, TENNESSEE
DESIGN AND ART DIRECTION BY BUDDY JACKSON AND HEATHER DRYDEN.

ISBN: 1-555853-932-8

PRINTED IN THE UNITED STATES OF AMERICA
01 02 03 04 05 – 5 4 3 2 1

IN MEMORY OF:
JUANITA puckitt keen
ROBERT and Earl keen, SR.

★ MERRY CHRISTMAS ·

MOM got drunk & DAD got drunk
at our CHRISTMAS party
we were drinking champagne PUNCH
And homade EGG nog
little sister BROUGHT her new Boyfriend
HE was a MEXICAN
we didn't KNOW what to THINK of him
'Til HE Sang FELIZ NAViDAD
FELIZ Marividad

BROTHER Ken brought His kids with Him
the 3 from His first wife LYNN
and the 2 identical twins
FROM his 2nd wife MARY NELL
of course HE BROUGHT his new wife KAY
who tALks all about AA
chain smokin' while the stereo plays
NOEL, noel, the First Noel

carve the turkey turn the ball game on
mix margaritas when the egg nog's gone
send somebody to the Quick Pak store
we NEED some ice & AN extension cord
a CAN of bean DIP and some Diet Rite
a box of TAMPONS & some marlboro lights
hallelujah everbody say CHEEZE
merry Christmas from the family

FROM THE FAMILY

Fran and Rita drove from Harlingen
I can't REMEMBER how i'm kin to them
but when they tried to plug their motor home in
they blew our Christmas lights
cousin David knew just what went wrong
So we all waited on our front lawn
he threw a BREAKER and the lights came on
and we sang SILENT NIGHT

on silent night
Oh Holy Night,

carve the turkey turn THE ball game on
mix margaritas when the egg nogs GONE
send somebody to the QUIK-PAK store
We need some ice AND an extention cord
a can of BEAN dip & some diet-rite
A box of tampons and some Marlboro lights
hallelujah everbody say cheese
Merry Christmas from the FAM-O-LEE

carve the turkey turn the BALL GAME on
make BLOODY MARYS cause we All want one
Send somebody to the STOP N' GO
We need SOME CELERY & a can of fake snow
a bag of Lemons & some diet SPRITE
A box of tampons and some SALEM lites
HALLELUJAH, everbody say CHEESE
Merry Christmas from the FAM-O-LEE

Feliz Navidad

WHITEWAY
49¢

mom got drunk and dad got drunk
at ouR christmas party . . .

PUNCH

Champagne punch

HOMEMADE

1/2 CUP LIGHT RUM

1/2 CUP DARK RUM

1/2 CUP FRESH Lemon juice

1 CUP FRESH orange juice

1 CUP PINE-APPLE juice

1/2 CUP SUGAR

2 BOTTLES of Champagne

Directions:

IN a 3-QUART BOWL, MIX RUMS, JUICES, AND SUGAR. CHILL.

WHEN ready to serve STIR IN CHAMPAGNE! GARNISH with orange & lemon slices

CHILLED ORANGE AND lemon SLICES.

EGGNOG
→ FROM HELL

3 OF THEM CARTONS
OF EGGNOG

1 CARTON OF THE
your
LIQUOR OF CHOICE.
(NO BIGGER THAN THE
CARTON OF EGGNOG!
(make mine *everclear*)

NOTE: IF THE LIQUOR OF
YOUR CHOICE IS CLEAR
AND NOT TOO HEAVILY
FLAVORED, MOST OF
THE GUESTS WON'T
KNOW HOW CHEAP
YOU ARE! IF YOU TRY
TO THROW IN YER
LEFTOVER PEPPERMINT
SCHNAPPS OR SLOE GIN,
IT AIN'T GONNA WORK
TOO WELL.

GET A BIG PITCHER
OR PUNCH BOWL.
▷ MIX ALL INGREDIENTS.

FER A SMALLER PORTION

1 CARTON OF EGGNOG
(POUR OUT ONE GLASS
& FEED TO THE
NEIGHBOR'S CAT)

POUR INTO THE CARTON
ENOUGH **LIQUOR**
OF YOUR CHOICE TO ALMOST
FILL the Carton, BUT
LEAVE A LITTLE ROOM
TO STIR IT UP.
THIS WAY YOU DON'T
NEED A SEPARATE
CONTAINER. PLUS
IT'S PORTABLE IF
CHURCH IS RUNNING
TOO LONG.

▷ DON'T USE A METAL CONTAIN-
CUZ IF THE LIQUOR'S TOO ER
STRONG, IT'LL EAT THRU THE BOWL.

FER *fancy eggnog:*
POUR INTO STYROFOAM
CUPS.
garnish with sprinkle
of ~~eg~~ NUTMEG.

OTHER FUN FAMILY
DRINKS *by AK"*

① GATORITA - GATORADE
(PREFERABLY original lime)
and Tequila. (Be sure
and use the wide mouth Bottle)
(this is great for camping!)

→ ② INSTANT ASTRONAUT -
Tang & Vodka (no water
what an eye-needed)
opener!

③ BEER — you can try this at home.
SHOT

✦ ④. BRISKY SOUR — canned lemon ice tea
and bourbon.

Little sister
brought her new boyfriend.

He was a Mexican.
We didn't know what to think of him

feliz navidad
feliz navidad
feliz navidad
prospero ano y felicidad
feliz navidad
feliz navidad
feliz navidad
prospero ano y felicidad
i wanna wish you a
merry christmas
i wanna wish you a
merry christmas
i wanna wish youpa
merry christmas
from the bottom of my
heart

FYI

THIS SONG IS BEST SUNG WHILE WEARING ONE OF THOSE GIANT STRAW MEXICAN SOMBREROS THAT NO MEXICAN WOULD BE CAUGHT DEAD WEARING. ALSO, WHEN YOU COME TO "I WANT TO WISH YOU A MERRY CHRISTMAS," SCREAM IT OUT LIKE YOU'RE TRYING TO BE HEARD WORLDWIDE.

The three from his
first wife Lynn

IN GUAD WE TRUST

And the two identical twins

Of course he
brought his
new wife Kay

who **talks all**
about **AA**

DUE TO INCREASING PRODUCT LIABILITY LITIGATION, AMERICAN BEER BREWERS HAVE ACCEPTED THE FDA'S SUGGESTION THAT THE FOLLOWING WARNING LABELS BE PLACED IMMEDIATELY ON ALL BEER CONTAINERS:

WARNING: THE CONSUMPTION OF ALCOHOL MAY CAUSE YOU TO THINK YOU CAN SING.

WARNING: THE CONSUMPTION OF ALCOHOL MAY LEAD YOU TO BELIEVE THAT EX-LOVERS ARE REALLY DYING FOR YOU TO TELEPHONE THEM AT FOUR IN THE MORNING.

WARNING: THE CONSUMPTION OF ALCOHOL MAY MAKE YOU MISTAKENLY THINK YOU CAN CONVERSE WITH MEMBERS OF THE OPPOSITE SEX WITHOUT SPITTING ALL OVER THEM.

WARNING: THE CONSUMPTION OF ALCOHOL MAY MAKE YOU THINK YOU HAVE MYSTICAL KUNG FU POWERS, RESULTING IN YOUR GETTING YOUR ASS KICKED.

WARNING: THE CONSUMPTION OF ALCOHOL IS THE LEADING CAUSE OF INEXPLICABLE RUG BURNS ON THE FOREHEAD.

WARNING: THE CONSUMPTION OF ALCOHOL MAY CAUSE PREGNANCY.

The first Noel, the angels did say,
Was to certain poor shepards in fields as they lay;
In fields where they lay keeping their sheep,
On a cold winter's night that was so deep.
No-el, No-el, No-el, No-el,
Born is the King of Israel.

They looked up and saw a star
Shining in the East, beyond them far,
And to the earth it gave great light,
And so it continued, both day and night.
No-el, No-el, No-el, No-el,
Born is the King of Israel.

RU

BREAST

THIGH

THREE REASONS NOT TO CARVE A TURKEY WHEN DRUNK

1. YOU WILL NEED YOUR INDEX FINGER IF YOU EVER PLAN ON TWIRLING A BATON, OR IMITATING JOHN TRAVOLTA IN *SATURDAY NIGHT FEVER,* OR ON FIRING A GUN.

2. JUST BECAUSE THE KNIFE YOU BOUGHT ON THE TELEVISION SHOPPING CHANNEL WILL CUT THROUGH BONE IS NO REASON TO TRY IT.

3. YOUR MAMMA WILL NEVER FORGIVE YOU IF YOU GET BLOOD ON THE HANDMADE CHRISTMAS TABLECLOTH HER AUNT WILMA BROUGHT BACK FROM MEXICO CITY.

LEG

LEG

GIZZARD

SING ALONG!

Let your voices rise with unparalleled reckless abandon.

Turn the ball game on

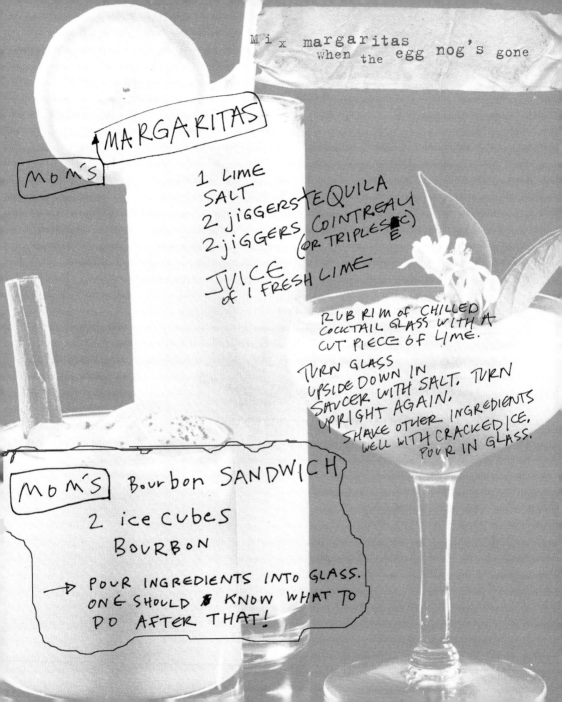

Mom's MARGARITAS

1 LIME
SALT
2 JIGGERS TEQUILA
2 JIGGERS COINTREAU
(OR TRIPLE SEC)
JUICE of 1 FRESH LIME

RUB RIM OF CHILLED
COCKTAIL GLASS WITH A
CUT PIECE OF LIME.

TURN GLASS
UPSIDE DOWN IN
SAUCER WITH SALT. TURN
UPRIGHT AGAIN.
SHAKE OTHER INGREDIENTS
WELL WITH CRACKED ICE.
POUR IN GLASS.

Mom's Bourbon SANDWICH

2 ice cubes
BOURBON

POUR INGREDIENTS INTO GLASS.
ONE SHOULD KNOW WHAT TO
DO AFTER THAT!

A can of bean dip and some Diet Rite,
A box of Tampons and some Marlboro Lights.

[ACTUAL SIZE]

TAMPON ANGEL
(PLAYTEX TAMPONS WORK BEST BECAUSE THEY EXPAND INTO A CONE SHAPE)

1. DIP INTO WATER UNTIL THE TAMPON EXPANDS.
2. REMOVE FROM WATER AND TIE THE STRING AT THE TOP TO CREATE THE ANGEL'S HEAD.
3. HANG THE TAMPON BY ITS STRING FOR SEVERAL DAYS UNTIL DRY.
4. PAINT THE FACE WITH PEACH-COLORED PAINT AND MAKE SMALL BLACK DOTS FOR EYES AFTER THE SKIN PAINT IS DRY.
5. ADD BLUSH TO CHEEKS.
6. PAINT THE DRESS WITH GLIMMER PAINT OR ADD GLITTER.
7. TIE A THIN GOLD RIBBON AROUND THE NECK.
8. ADD DOLL HAIR ON TOP OF THE HEAD AND A PIPE CLEANER FOR THE HALO.
9. GLUE SMALL GOLD OR SILVER ANGEL WINGS ON THE BACK.

EVERYBODY SAY
"CHEEEEZE!"

Halle

Hallelujah.
        Everybody say cheese.

ujah!

ese

KEN
SIS
DAD
Fran
MERRY
christMAS

MOM

Kay

Rita

KIDS

WINS

FROM the
FAM-O-lEE!

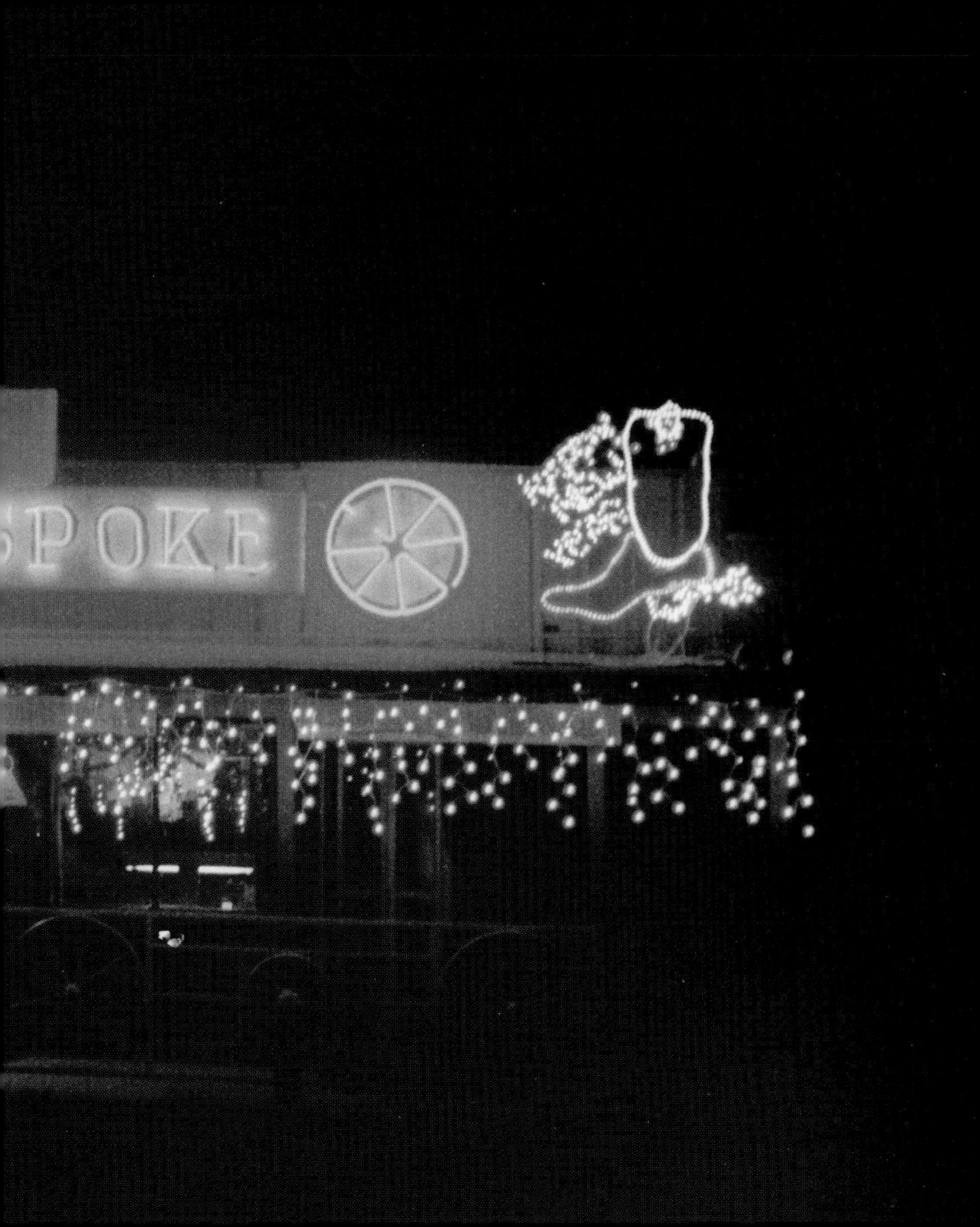
SPOKE

Fran and Rita drove from Harlingen.

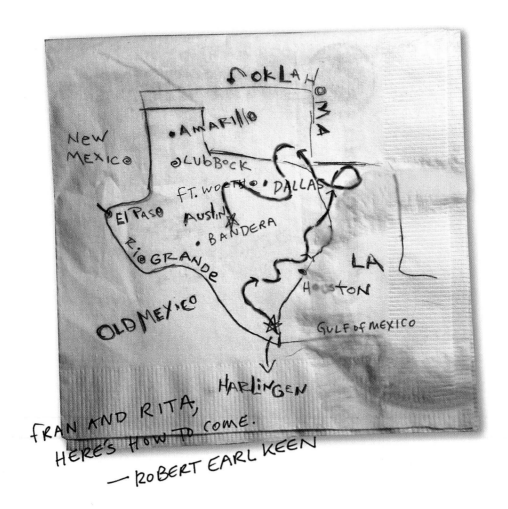

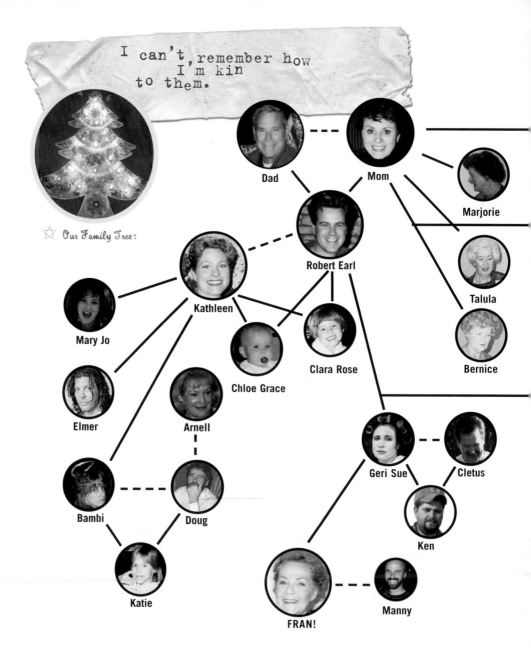

I can't remember how I'm kin to them.

☆ Our Family Tree:

Dad
Mom
Marjorie
Robert Earl
Talula
Kathleen
Bernice
Mary Jo
Clara Rose
Chloe Grace
Elmer
Arnell
Geri Sue
Cletus
Bambi
Doug
Ken
Katie
FRAN!
Manny

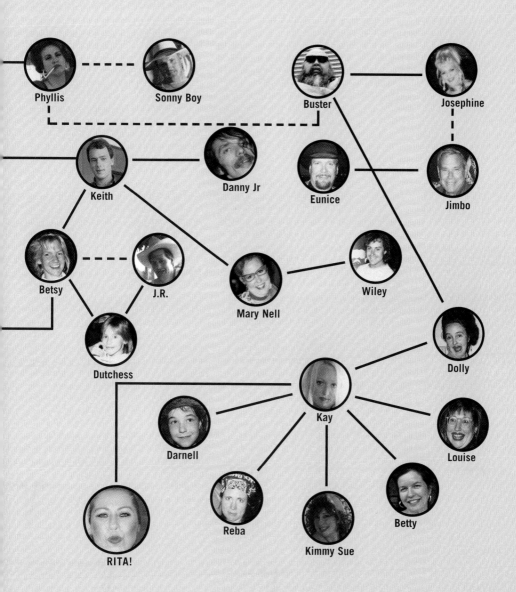

But when they tried to plug their motor home in...

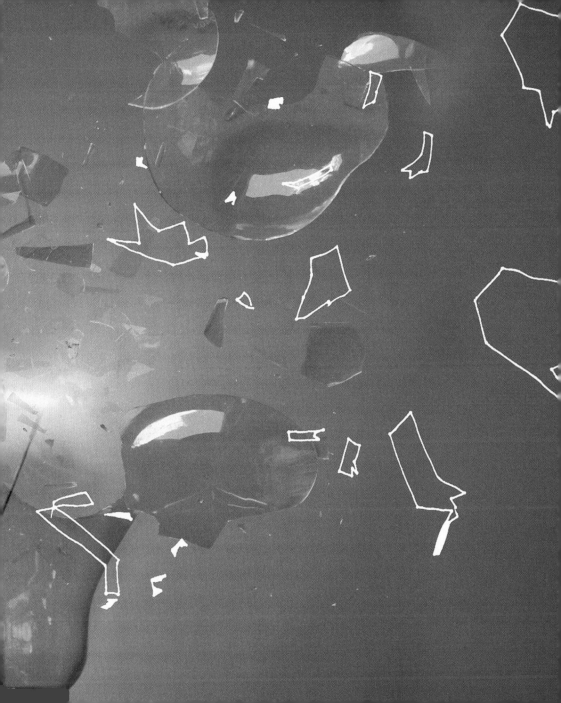

Cousin david knew just what went wrong.

So we all waited out on our front lawn.

He threw a breaker and
the Lights came on.

And we sang
siLENT **NIGHT!** OH SILENT NIGHT...
OH HOLY NIGHT...

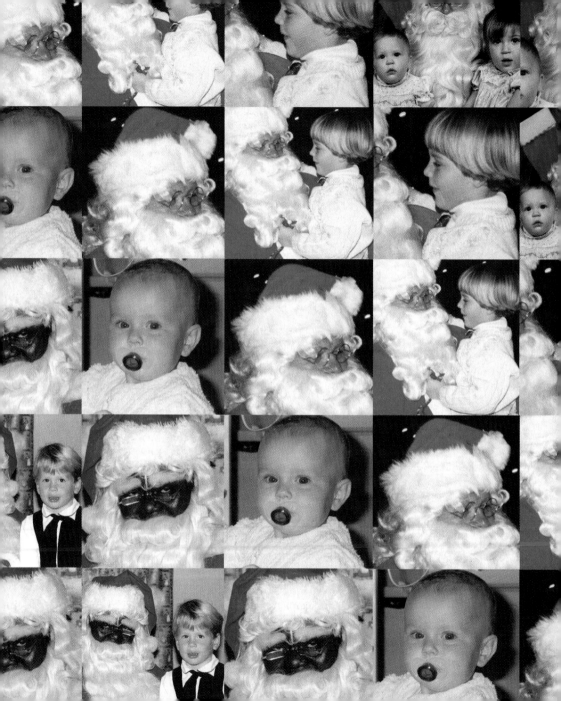

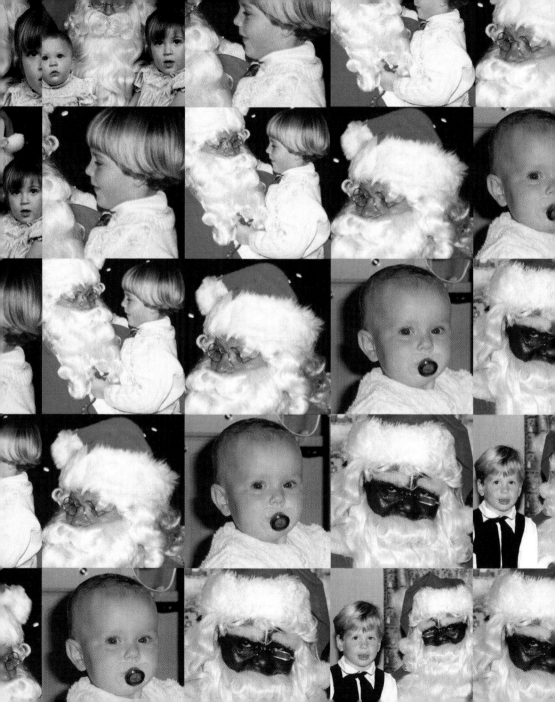

nce upon a time, in a far distant land there lived a beautiful Christmas turkey named Timmy. Now Timmy was beautiful but he was very small and all the other turkeys picked on him. They ridiculed Timmy and made fun of him in front of the girl turkeys.

That was, of course, until Christmas time came around and all them fat turkeys

had their big heads on the chopping block.
THEN whose turn was it to laugh?
That's right,
fat
boy!

Timmy
the
Christmas
turkey got the
LAST LAUGH!

THE END!

MAKE Bloody MARYs

"BLOODY MARY"
"JOLLY STYLE"

½ glass Hot n' spicy V8 juice
½ glass Clamato juice
1 pinch Horse radish
1 dash   Worcestershire sauce
1 dash   Tabasco sauce
1 tsp.   Olive juice
1 pinch Celery salt
1 pinch Pepper

1 Shot Vodka

Add together in a glass,
and stir. Garnish with a
lemon or lime wedge,
chunk of cheese and
an olive.

christmas

text by papaw
photographs by mamaw

martha's celebrity celery sticks

Holiday time is here, and what more exciting addition to your holiday spread than the celery sticks served at the tables of *your* favorite celebrity?

When the family and friends gather around the fire and the aroma of cinnamon and nutmeg is in the air, what's the topic on everyone's mind? Food. And for an especially scrumptous holiday, the staple of any successful holiday feast is the festive flavor of fresh celery topped with a varity of scrumptous fillings. This year forget the traditional cream cheese or pimento cheese stuffings. Martha has gone all out this year, gathering up the celery stick recipes that her famous friends serve at their own holiday gatherings. So whether your family wishes a Merry Christmas, Happy Hannuka or Cheery Kwanza for your loved ones, impress them all with Martha's Celebrity Celery Sticks.

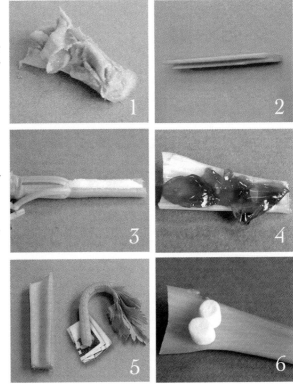

recipes

1	ELVIS peanut butter and bacon
2	ALI McCELERY really skinny celery
3	ROBERT DOWNEY JR white powder
4	JENNIFER LOPEZ J-Lo
5	ANNA NICOLE SMITH & HUSBAND sugar daddy
6	PAMELA ANDERSON marshmallows
7	RONALD REAGAN uh, well, I forgot

And a can
of fake snow

10 things to do
WITH FAKE SN

A bag of lemons and
some Diet Sprite A box of tampons and some
salem lights.

Y → 10. SPRAY-ON Halter top

9. COVER Grandpa's BALD SPOT

8. FAKE POLAR BEAR RUG

7. SPRAY-ON Gift wrap

6. HIDE A MOUNTAIN of UNPAID BILLS

5. ACOUSTIC TOUCH UP

4. DECORATE Billy Bass

3. AN INSTANT AFRO

2. cookie icing (do not try this at home)

#1. eye shadow

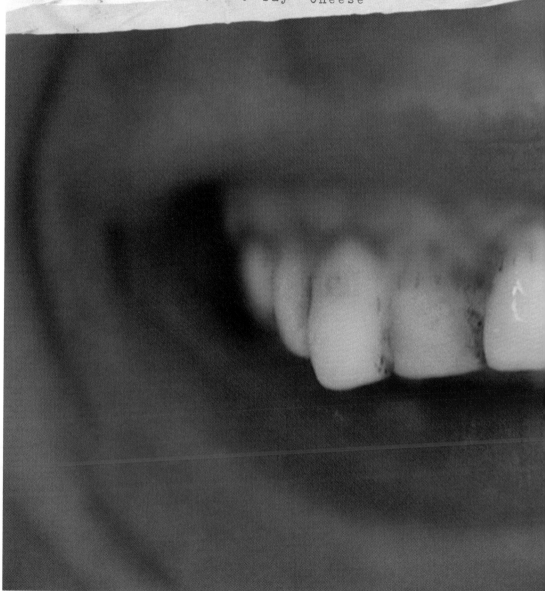

Hallelujah!
Everybody say "Cheese"

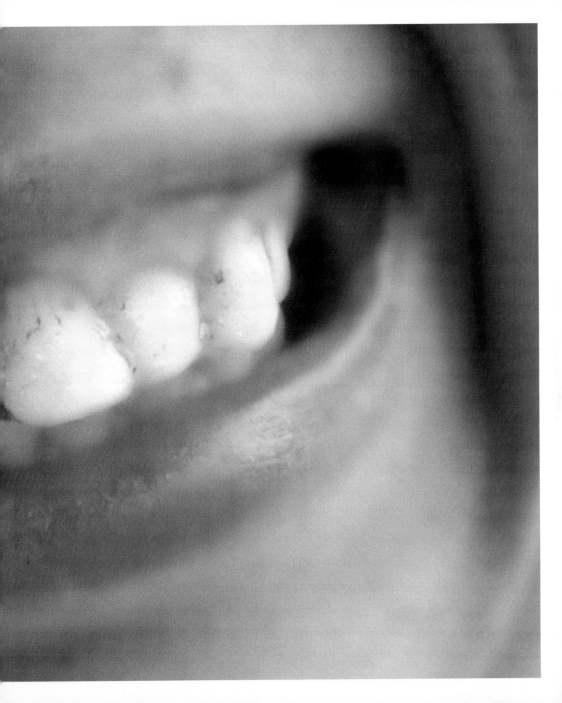

Merry Christmas FROM the FAM-O-lEE!

Feliz Navidad!

Merry Christmas

Merry Christmas